Best Free Open S

Software For Windows 10

Bilingual Edition English Germany

by

Cyber Jannah Sakura

2021

Prologue

The Complete List of Free Opensource Office Suite Software Available on Windows 10 For School, College, Research, Work and Business. Bilingual Edition In English and Germany Languange.

Die vollständige Liste der kostenlosen Opensource Office Suite Software auf Windows 10 für Schule, Hochschule, Forschung, Arbeit und Business. Zweisprachige Ausgabe In Englisch und Deutsch Sprache.

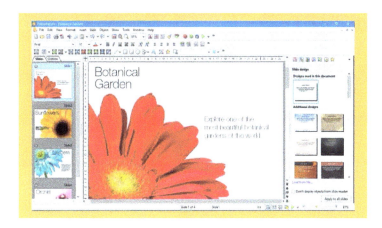

Chapter 2 English Version

List of Free Opensource Office Suite Software Available on Windows 10 English Version

1. Calligra Suite

Calligra Suite is an office and graphic art suite by KDE. It is available for desktop PCs, tablet computers, and smartphones.

It contains applications for word processing, spreadsheets, presentation, vector graphics, and editing databases.

www.calligra.org

2. Apache OpenOffice

Apache OpenOffice is the leading open-source office software suite for word processing, spreadsheets, presentations, graphics, databases and more. It is available in many languages and works on all common computers.

It stores all your data in an international open standard format and can also read and write files from other common office software packages. It can be downloaded and used completely free of charge for any purpose.

www.openoffice.org

3. Libre Office

Libre Office is a free and open-source office suite software, a project of The Document Foundation. It was forked in 2010 from OpenOffice.org, which was an open-sourced version of the earlier Star Office Suite.

The Libre Office suite consists of programs for word processing, creating and editing of spreadsheets, slideshows, diagrams and drawings, working with databases, and composing mathematical formulae.

Libre Office also supports the file formats of most other major office suites, including Microsoft Office, through a variety of import and export filters.

www.libreoffice.org

4. Only Office

Only Office, stylized as ONLY OFFICE, is a free software office suite developed by Ascensio System SIA, a company headquartered in Riga, Latvia. It features online and offline document editors, platform for document management, corporate communication, mail and project management tools.

Only Office Desktop is an offline version of Only Office editing suite software. Desktop application supports collaborative editing features when connected to the portal, Nextcloud or ownCloud. Application is offered free of charge for both personal and commercial usage.

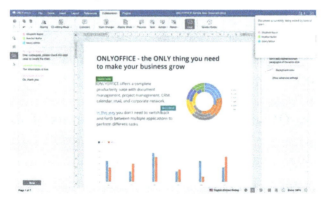

Desktop editors are cross-platform available for Windows 10, 8.1, 8, 7, Vista, and XP (x32 and x64), Debian, Ubuntu and other Linux distributions based on RPM, Mac OS 10.10 and newer.

Besides platform-specific versions there is also a portable option. OnlyOffice Desktop Editors are available for installation as a snap package and AppImage.

www.onlyoffice.com

5. AbiWord

AbiWord is a free and open-source software word processor. It is written in C++ and since version 3 it is based on GTK+ 3. The name "AbiWord" is derived from the root of the Spanish word "abierto", meaning "open".

AbiWord was originally started by SourceGear Corporation as the first part of a proposed AbiSuite but was adopted by open source developers after SourceGear changed its business focus and ceased development.

It now runs on Linux, ReactOS, Solaris, AmigaOS 4.0 (through its Cygwin X11 engine), MeeGo (on the Nokia N9 smartphone), Maemo (on the Nokia N810) QNX and other operating systems. AbiWord is part of the AbiSource project which develops a number of office-related technologies.

www.abisource.com

6. WPS Office

WPS Office is an office suite for Microsoft Windows, macOS, Linux, iOS and Android .Developed by Zhuhai-based Chinese software developer Kingsoft.

WPS Office is made up of three primary components: WPS Writer, WPS Presentation, and WPS Spreadsheet.

The personal basic version is free to use. A fully featured professional-grade version is also available for a subscription fee.

WPS Office 2016 was released in 2016. As of 2019, the Linux version is developed and supported by a volunteer community rather than Kingsoft itself.

By 2019, WPS Office reached a number of more than 310 milion monthly active users.

The product has had a long history of development in China under the name "WPS" and "WPS Office". For a time, Kingsoft branded the suite as "KSOffice" in an attempt to gain an international market foothold, but later returned to "WPS Office".

Since WPS Office 2005 the user interface is similar to that of Microsoft Office products, and supports Microsoft document formats besides native Kingsoft formats.

www.wps.com

7. SoftMaker FreeOffice

SoftMaker Office is an office suite developed since 1987 by the German company SoftMaker Software GmbH based in Nuremberg. SoftMaker is available as a one-time purchase option, in Standard and Professional editions, as well as a subscription-based version known as SoftMaker Office NX (available as Home and Universal editions).

A freeware version is released as well, under the name of SoftMaker FreeOffice. FreeOffice supersedes SoftMaker Office 2006 and 2008, which were released as freeware.

SoftMaker Office has similar functionality to other office suites such as Microsoft Office or LibreOffice, and can also run from USB flash drives and supports integrated reference works.

Multi-language spell-checking, hyphenation and thesaurus is supported, and it has an integrated five-language translation dictionary (English, German, French, Italian, and Spanish).

It has its own native formats, and can read and write file formats of Microsoft Office, OpenDocument format (word processor only), RTF and HTML.

Support for the OpenDocument spreadsheet (ODS) format was added in the Anniversary update released for SoftMaker Office 2018. It can export to PDF and EPUB.

The user interface is similar to the Ribbon utilized in Microsoft Office 2007 and later, and there is an option to use menus and toolbars instead of the Ribbon. A dark mode is available. Documents can be opened as tabs in a single window, to allow easy switching between multiple documents.

www.freeoffice.com

Chapter 3 Germany Version

Liste der kostenlosen Opensource-Office-Suite-Software, die unter Windows 10 Deutschland Version verfügbar ist.

1. Calligra Suite

Die Calligra Suite ist eine Büro- und Grafiksuite von KDE. Es ist für Desktop-PCs, Tablet-Computer und Smartphones verfügbar.

Es enthält Anwendungen für Textverarbeitung, Tabellenkalkulationen, Präsentationen, Vektorgrafiken und das Bearbeiten von Datenbanken.

www.calligra.org

2. Apache OpenOffice

Apache OpenOffice ist die führende Open-Source-Office-Software-Suite für Textverarbeitung, Tabellenkalkulationen, Präsentationen, Grafiken, Datenbanken und mehr. Es ist in vielen Sprachen verfügbar und funktioniert auf allen gängigen Computern.

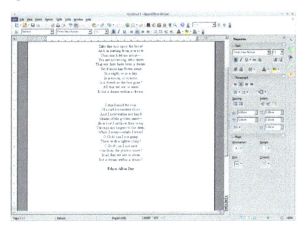

Es speichert alle Ihre Daten in einem internationalen offenen Standardformat und kann auch Dateien aus anderen gängigen Office-Softwarepaketen lesen und schreiben. Es kann für jeden Zweck völlig kostenlos heruntergeladen und verwendet werden.

www.openoffice.org

3. Libre Office

Libre Office ist eine kostenlose Open-Source-Office-Suite-Software, ein Projekt der Document Foundation. Es wurde 2010 von OpenOffice.org gespalten, einer Open-Source-Version der früheren Star Office Suite.

Die Libre Office-Suite besteht aus Programmen zur Textverarbeitung, zum Erstellen und Bearbeiten von Tabellenkalkulationen, Diashows, Diagrammen und Zeichnungen, zum Arbeiten mit Datenbanken und zum Erstellen mathematischer Formeln.

Als natives Dateiformat zum Speichern von Dokumenten für alle Anwendungen verwendet LibreOffice das Open Document Format für Office-Anwendungen (ODF) oder OpenDocument, einen internationalen Standard, der gemeinsam von der Internationalen Organisation für Normung (ISO) und der International Electrotechnical Commission (ISO) entwickelt wurde. IEC).

Libre Office unterstützt auch die Dateiformate der meisten anderen wichtigen Office-Suiten, einschließlich Microsoft Office, durch eine Vielzahl von Import- und Exportfiltern.

www.libreoffice.org

4. Only Office

Only Office, stilisiert als ONLY OFFICE, ist eine kostenlose Software-Office-Suite, die von Ascensio System SIA, einem Unternehmen mit Hauptsitz in Riga, Lettland, entwickelt wurde.

Only Office Desktop ist eine Offline-Version der Only Office Editing Suite-Software. Die Desktop-Anwendung unterstützt kollaborative Bearbeitungsfunktionen, wenn sie mit dem Portal.

Nextcloud oder ownCloud verbunden ist. Die Anwendung wird sowohl für den persönlichen als auch für den kommerziellen Gebrauch kostenlos angeboten.

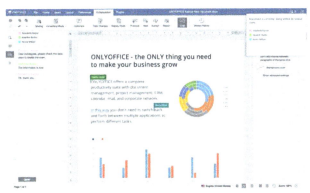

Desktop-Editoren sind plattformübergreifend für Windows 10, 8.1, 8, 7, Vista und XP (x32 und x64), Debian, Ubuntu und andere Linux-Distributionen verfügbar, die auf RPM, Mac OS 10.10 und neuer basieren.

Neben plattformspezifischen Versionen gibt es auch eine tragbare Option. OnlyOffice Desktop Editors können als Snap-Paket und AppImage installiert werden.

www.onlyoffice.com

5. AbiWord

AbiWord ist ein kostenloses Open-Source-Software-Textverarbeitungsprogramm. Es ist in C ++ geschrieben und basiert seit Version 3 auf GTK + 3. Der Name „AbiWord" leitet sich von der Wurzel des spanischen Wortes „abierto" ab und bedeutet „offen".

AbiWord wurde ursprünglich von der SourceGear Corporation als erster Teil einer vorgeschlagenen AbiSuite gestartet, aber von Open Source-Entwicklern übernommen, nachdem SourceGear seinen Geschäftsfokus geändert und die Entwicklung eingestellt hatte.

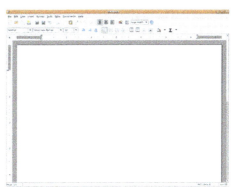

Es läuft jetzt unter Linux, ReactOS, Solaris, AmigaOS 4.0 (über die Cygwin X11-Engine), MeeGo (auf dem Nokia N9-Smartphone), Maemo (auf dem Nokia N810), QNX und anderen Betriebssystemen. AbiWord ist Teil des AbiSource-Projekts, das eine Reihe von Bürotechnologien entwickelt.

www.abisource.com

6. WPS Office

WPS Office ist eine Office-Suite für Microsoft Windows, MacOS, Linux, iOS und Android. Entwickelt von dem in Zhuhai ansässigen chinesischen Softwareentwickler Kingsoft. WPS Office besteht aus drei Hauptkomponenten: WPS Writer, WPS Presentation und WPS Spreadsheet.

Die persönliche Basisversion ist kostenlos. Gegen eine Abonnementgebühr ist auch eine voll funktionsfähige Professional-Version erhältlich.

WPS Office 2016 wurde 2016 veröffentlicht. Ab 2019 wird die Linux-Version von einer freiwilligen Community und nicht von Kingsoft selbst entwickelt und unterstützt. Bis 2019 erreichte WPS Office eine Anzahl von mehr als 310 Millionen aktiven Benutzern pro Monat.

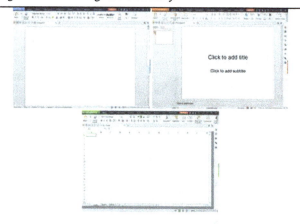

Das Produkt hat in China eine lange Entwicklungsgeschichte unter den Namen „WPS" und „WPS Office". Kingsoft bezeichnete die Suite eine Zeit lang als „KSOffice", um auf dem internationalen Markt Fuß zu fassen, kehrte jedoch später zu „WPS Office" zurück.

Seit WPS Office 2005 ähnelt die Benutzeroberfläche der von Microsoft Office-Produkten und unterstützt neben nativen Kingsoft-Formaten auch Microsoft-Dokumentformate.

www.wps.com

7. SoftMaker FreeOffice

SoftMaker Office ist eine Office-Suite, die seit 1987 von der deutschen Firma SoftMaker Software GmbH mit Sitz in Nürnberg entwickelt wurde. SoftMaker ist als einmalige Kaufoption in Standard- und Professional-Editionen sowie als abonnementbasierte Version mit der Bezeichnung SoftMaker Office NX (als Home- und Universal-Edition erhältlich) erhältlich.

Unter dem Namen SoftMaker FreeOffice wird auch eine Freeware-Version veröffentlicht. FreeOffice ersetzt SoftMaker Office 2006 und 2008, die als Freeware veröffentlicht wurden.

SoftMaker Office bietet ähnliche Funktionen wie andere Office-Suiten wie Microsoft Office oder LibreOffice. Es kann auch von USB-Sticks ausgeführt werden und unterstützt integrierte Nachschlagewerke.

Die Benutzeroberfläche ähnelt der in Microsoft Office 2007 und höher verwendeten Multifunktionsleiste. Außerdem können Sie anstelle der Multifunktionsleiste Menüs und Symbolleisten verwenden. Ein dunkler Modus ist verfügbar.

Dokumente können als Registerkarten in einem einzigen Fenster geöffnet werden, um das einfache Wechseln zwischen mehreren Dokumenten zu ermöglichen.

www.freeoffice.com

References

Waterhouse, Shirley A. (1 January 1979). Word processing fundamentals. Canfield Press. ISBN 9780064537223.

Hinojosa, Santiago (1 June 2016). "The History of Word Processors". The Tech Ninja's Dojo.

Meeks, Michael (9 May 2011). "LibreOffice is the future of Free Software Office suites". Michael Meeks' blog at people.gnome.org. gnome.org

Brian Walsh (1996). "Business Computer Language". IT-Directors.com.

Peyton Jones, Simon; Burnett, Margaret; Blackwell, Alan (March 2003). "Improving the world's most popular functional language: user-defined functions in Excel"

Max Henrion (2004-07-14). "What's Wrong with Spreadsheets – and How to Fix them with Analytica"

Stephen Bullen, Rob Bovey & John Green (2009). Professional Excel Development (2nd ed.). Addison-Wesley. ISBN 978-0-321-50879-9.